D1317196

the teddy bear story

by Pat Rush

illustrated by Isobel Bushell

MQP

CONTENTS

teddy history

The teddy bear got its name from American President Theodore ('Teddy') Roosevelt. In November 1902 Roosevelt, a keen hunter, embarked on a four-day bear hunt in Mississippi, but during the whole time he failed to shoot a single bear. Other members of his party, however, managed to pursue and capture one. They tied it to a tree and sent for the president to give him the chance to make a kill. But Roosevelt refused to shoot the poor animal, nor would he allow anyone else to.

The political cartoonist Clifford Berryman recorded the incident in one of his drawings, and two days later, on 16th November 1902, it was published as one of a montage of Berryman cartoons, on the front of *The Washington Post*. Readers of the paper were delighted and letters flooded in from people eager to see more of the bear.

B erryman's original drawing was of a large and clearly frightened real bear, but it soon evolved into an adorable little cub — much more like a teddy bear. Neither Roosevelt nor Berryman, however, used the term teddy bear. Roosevelt called the little fellow the Berryman bear, and Berryman called him the Roosevelt bear. The term teddy bear was not used for a number of years, and did not appear in print until 1906.

Clifford Berryman's little bear soon became so much a part of his life that he included him in cartoons sent to family and friends. He even appeared on Christmas and birthday cards. He decorated letters and replies to invitations — suitably joyful, tearful or even totally tied up! Babies were welcomed by him, and he even found his way into Berryman's will — right beside his signature.

When Morris Michtom, a Russian immigrant living in the US, saw the famous cartoon of President Roosevelt and the bear in *The Washington Post*, he asked his wife Rose if she could make a toy bear that looked like the one in the drawing. Rose did so, and they put the little animal in the window of their shop in Brooklyn, New York. It was a huge success.

They made another and another, but the bears sold as soon as they were put in the window. In response to the huge demand

Morris and Rose Michtom set up their own toy-making company, which they called the Ideal Novelty and Toy Company. This was to grow from these humble beginnings into a vast multi-million dollar corporation.

Michtom claimed that he wrote to President Roosevelt asking his permission to name the little bear Teddy. The president is said to have agreed in a hand-written reply — although this letter has never been found.

Although it was an American president that gave the teddy bear its name, it is possible that the very first teddy bear was made by a German company — that founded by Margarete Steiff.

Margarete Steiff's company had been making toy animals, including bears, for a number of years by 1902, but the bears were unjointed, and looked very much like real bears. It was not until Margarete's nephew Richard Steiff went along to watch some performing bears in a visiting circus (on 21st October 1902), that the idea for a jointed bear arose. Richard had been fascinated by bears since his days as an art student in Stuttgart, and it was while watching the performing bears that he was inspired to design what many believe to have been the very first teddy bear.

Steiff are still making teddy bears today, and early ones are much coveted by collectors.

Steiff's first jointed bear became known as the 55 PB — 55 being its size in centimetres, the P standing for plush and the B for *beweglich*, or jointed. It received its official launch at the Leipzig Trade Fair in March 1903. Although other Steiff toys proved as popular as ever, curiously the bear was not an instant success.

Then, right at the end of the fair, an American wholesaler visited the stand, complaining that he couldn't find anything really different to take back to New York with him. He was shown the new bear, and promptly ordered 3,000 of them.

B y the time Theodore Roosevelt campaigned for re-election in 1904, he had become so associated with bears in the minds of the public that the Republican Party decided to capitalise on the link. As Roosevelt toured the country in his special campaign train, toy bears were handed out to the people who crowded round to see him. A special campaign badge, with a tiny teddy suspended from it, was also made.

Even after his presidency ended, the association continued. When Roosevelt visited Britain in 1910, students at Cambridge University welcomed him by placing a small teddy in his path, with its paw stretched out in greeting.

B Y 1906, THE WHOLE OF AMERICA HAD BEEN GRIPPED BY TEDDY BEAR FEVER. SOME BEARS WERE MADE IN THE US, BUT THE GERMAN COMPANY STEIFF WAS ALSO ENJOYING ENORMOUS SUCCESS THERE — WITH UP TO 90% OF ITS BEARS BEING SOLD TO AMERICAN CUSTOMERS. THE YEARS 1906–14 WERE BOOM YEARS FOR STEIFF BEARS. IN 1907 NO FEWER THAN 975,000 LEFT THE FACTORY — A FIGURE YET TO BE EQUALLED.

As the popularity of the teddy bear increased, competition between manufacturers grew fierce, with many creating ingenious novelties to attract customers.

Several American companies exploited the Roosevelt connection. Columbia Teddy Bear Manufacturers in New York advertised a Laughing Teddy Bear that, like Roosevelt, laughed and showed his teeth, and another New York company, the American Doll and Toy Manufacturing Company, offered 'White House' teddy bears.

Other companies were even more inventive. G.C. Gillespie offered tumbling bears with concealed weights that could somersault down sloping planks; the Strauss company had a Self-Whistling Bear with a mechanism inside his body that made

him whistle when he was turned upside down; and the Fast Black Skirt Co. devised an Electric Bright Eye Teddy Bear whose eyes lit up when his right paw was shaken.

Steiff, too, made a somersaulting bear; they also produced a teddy string puppet, known as the Phantom Bear, and, in 1907, a hot water bottle bear. This bear was designed so that a hot water bottle made of steel could be laced up inside it to keep a child warm at night, while during the day the bear could be played with as usual. Steiff were sure that this would be a huge success as the previous winter had been especially cold, but unfortunately the idea failed to catch on and over the next seven years only 90 were sold.

Steiff bears evolved rapidly during the early years of the company. The first to be made was very weighty, with joints made from a heavy twine. No one is quite sure what he looked like — no examples have ever been found, none have been preserved in the company's archives and only an old catalogue photograph remains.

This bear was followed by a smaller, improved design which was known simply as the 35 PB. Although thousands were sold, Steiff were still not satisfied. The twine-jointed limbs soon became loose, and a new system of jointing the bears by means of metal rods was developed. Today these Steiff 'rod' bears are highly collectable. An x-ray of the bear will clearly show the position of the internal rods, as a number of proud owners have discovered.

Steiff continued to work at improving their bears, and the rod joints were soon replaced by disc jointing which is still used in bears today.

Steiff was, and is, the most famous of all the German bear manufacturers, although within a few years the country's great bear-making region was the Sonneberg-Neustadt area, 200 miles away — already well-known for its other toys.

In Sonneberg, toy making was very much a cottage industry. There were numerous small manufacturers, each employing teams of outworkers to make up toys in their own homes. Whole families worked on the bears together, with children as young as ten years old often working ten or twelve hours a day. Most of these bears were exported to the US, but some of the cheaper designs were sold to German amusement parks, where they were given away as prizes.

L ike German bears, early British bears often had long arms, large feet, protruding muzzles and humps on their backs. The London firm J.K. Farnell began making bears sometime between 1906 and 1908, and may have been the first British company to do so, although German bears had been imported to Britain for several years. Early advertisements for British bears pointed out their similarity to their German cousins — a practice which ended abruptly with the outbreak of the First World War.

The First World War resulted in a boom for the British teddy bear and soft toy industry. Because German imports were no longer available, British companies stepped in to fill the gap. They also stopped imitating the style of German bears and the limbs of British bears became shorter, the noses less pronounced, the humps disappeared and a softer, altogether friendlier, type of bear began to develop.

Patriotic mascot teddies were also popular during the War. London-based Harwin & Co. Ltd (founded in 1914) produced a whole range of Ally Bears dressed in the uniforms of Britain's allies. One of the most popular designs was a bear in a flared tunic and puttees. Others included a jaunty sailor and a Red Cross nurse.

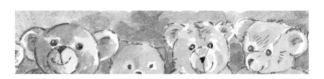

THE YEARS BETWEEN THE WARS WERE A

BOOM TIME FOR THE BRITISH SOFT TOY

INDUSTRY. BY THE 1930S IT WAS CLAIMED

THAT MORE SOFT TOYS WERE BEING MADE IN

SHROPSHIRE THAN ANYWHERE ELSE IN THE

WORLD. MORE, EVEN, THAN IN THE GREAT

TOY-MAKING AREAS OF GERMANY.

In America, a new style of bear began to appear during the 1920s and 30s — mass-produced and of a much poorer quality than the original American teddy bears. Known as stick bears, they had long thin bodies and short straight limbs, and were typically made from poor quality fur with short bristly pile. As the small factories which made them rarely attached any labels to their bears, the names of many of the makers are now long forgotten.

In Britain in the late 1920s, bears moved out of the nursery and became a popular fashion accessory. In 1931, for instance, the British company Merrythought were offering bears in 'Salmon, Ciel, Myosotis, Iris, Canary, Crimson, Copper-glow, and Jade', pointing out that these were 'the 1931 selections of the Paris Dress Designers'. The following year, they were offering the fashionable colours for 1932 — 'Eglantine, Azure, Copper, Red, Gold, Mimosa, Venus, and Clematis'.

I n 1939, there was 'pandamonium' in Britain following the arrival of a baby giant panda at London Zoo. The whole nation was captivated. Panda novelties such as brooches and hats began to appear, and soft toy companies cashed in on the craze, competing fiercely to produce the most original designs.

The London firm J.K. Farnell introduced a 'Glove Panda'; the famous Chad Valley Company introduced a wooden 'acrobatic walking panda bear' that could walk backwards or forwards; and the East London Toy Factory created panda nightdress cases, tea cosies, handbags, beach bags and knitting bags, as well as panda soft toys. They also made a panda with 'Sparklight electric eyes', operated by a hidden battery. But it was Merrythought's more realistic pandas which went on sale at London Zoo itself.

Not to be beaten, rival British company Dean's photographed the real panda inquisitively sniffing one of their Handy Pandy toys — and then used the picture in advertisements to support their claim that the two were constant companions and playmates!

During the Second World War, toy production by many companies almost ceased, as factories were taken over for other work. A shortage of materials both during and after the war led to bears being made from any cloth that was available. Precious fabric was saved by changing the design of the bears — faces became flatter, arms and legs were made shorter, and feet almost disappeared as manufacturers struggled to increase their output with limited resources.

After the Second World War, British bears continued to change as companies fought enormous competition posed by cheap imports from the Far East. Designs were simplified to reduce the costs of both materials and manufacture, with movable joints reserved only for the most expensive ranges and mohair increasingly replaced by cheaper synthetic fabrics. By the 1980s the traditional British teddy bear had almost disappeared.

B ear collecting on a wide scale is a relatively new phenome-non, and many of today's collectors believe that the British actor Peter Bull started it all. In the late 1960s, he placed an adver-tisement in *The Times* asking for information about the history of the teddy bear (or, as he put it, E. Bear Esquire). He invited peo-ple to send him reminiscences and photographs to be used in a book that he was planning to write.

He was swamped with replies — so many that he had to employ a secretary to deal with them. Other newspapers picked up the story. Peter appeared on radio and television on both sides of the Atlantic, and still more letters flooded in. He was not, he dis-covered, the only bear lover in the world. When his book *Bear with Me* was published in 1969, many others made the same discovery.

More bear books by Peter Bull appeared, each one bringing another avalanche of correspondence from like-minded souls. It became clear that the teddy bear was no longer just a children's toy; it had a whole new following amongst adults.

As more and more bear lovers started amassing huge collections of bruins, manufacturers found themselves with a whole new market. In the 1980s, several started making bears specifically for collectors, and because collectors like rarity, special limited-edition bears were introduced — each one individually numbered.

Steiff, for instance, began to delve into their archives and reproduce bears from their early catalogues. Other companies started to do the same. There were also new designs — for bears intended to be looked at by adults, not played with by children. Traditional jointed bears were, and still are, in great demand. A wide variety of dressed and character bears have also been created to attract the attention of the growing numbers of collectors.

T HE EARLY 1970S SAW THE APPEARANCE OF A NEW BREED OF TEDDY BEAR IN AMERICA — BEARS CREATED AS AN ART FORM RATHER THAN AS TOYS, AND MADE NOT IN FACTORIES BUT BY INDIVIDUAL CRAFTSPEOPLE IN THEIR HOMES. THESE BEARS BECAME KNOWN AS 'ARTIST BEARS', AND THE PEOPLE WHO MADE THEM WERE CALLED 'BEAR ARTISTS'.

THE FIRST BEAR ARTISTS WERE MAINLY DOLL DESIGNERS, AND THEIR BEARS WERE FIRST SEEN AT DOLL CONVENTIONS, ALTHOUGH THEY SOON BECAME POPULAR IN THEIR OWN RIGHT. TODAY THERE ARE HUNDREDS, POSSIBLY THOUSANDS, OF BEAR ARTISTS — NOT JUST IN AMERICA BUT ALL OVER THE WORLD.

In the early 1980s, London auction house Sotheby's included teddy bears in one of its toy sales. The highest price paid was less than £400. Now, teddies appear in a number of sales throughout the year, with a giant all-teddy sale at Christie's in London each December. By 1987, the world record price for a teddy bear (again sold at Sotheby's) was £8,800. In 1989 a bear was sold there for £55,000. Five years later, that record was dramatically broken by a bear called Teddy Girl sold at Christie's for no less than £110,000!

On 27th May 1979, a Great Teddy Bear Rally was held in England at Longleat, the home of the Marquis of Bath (himself a bear lover, and owner of a bespectacled bear called Clarence). It wasn't the first such gathering of bears and their owners; 1,500 teds had converged on a small Norfolk village some nine years earlier. The Longleat rally, however, sparked a succession of similar events all over the world, as well as innumerable smaller teddy bears' picnics. At these there were usually stalls selling bears and all sorts of bear-related items, as well as competitions with prizes for the oldest, smallest, saddest and most-loved bear.

Many teddy bears' picnics are still organised along the same lines today, although they now attract mainly the very young. Special collectors' fairs and conventions — some of them with hundreds of stalls — have greater appeal for today's collectors.

IN THE 1980s, MORE TEDDY BEARS WERE COL-LECTED IN THE US THAN ANYWHERE ELSE IN THE WORLD, ALTHOUGH COUNTRIES LIKE BRITAIN AND AUSTRALIA FOLLOWED CLOSELY BEHIND.

THERE ARE NOW MANY COLLECTORS IN GERMANY AND SEVERAL OTHER EUROPEAN COUN-TRIES. BEARS ARE ALSO ENJOYING ENORMOUS POPULARITY IN THE FAR EAST, ESPECIALLY IN JAPAN AND SINGAPORE. SOUTH AFRICA, TOO, HAS SEEN A GROWING NUMBER OF COLLECTORS AND BEAR MAKERS IN RECENT YEARS.

bear makers
past & present

The most famous bear manufacturer of all is the company founded by Margarete Steiff in the small town of Giengen in southern Germany.

Margarete Steiff suffered from polio as a child, which left her with no co-ordination in one arm, and confined to a wheelchair. Her disability didn't prevent her from becoming a talented needle-woman — she was the first person in Giengen to own a sewing machine, and she used this to make clothes for her family and friends. In 1877 she set up her own dressmaking company, where she made felt underskirts, dresses, coats and other garments.

She made her first toy, an elephant, from felt scraps using a pattern she found in a magazine. More were made as gifts for friends and, in 1880, she began to sell a small number. Soon other animals were introduced and within a few years she was making more toys than clothes.

The earliest Steiff bears were much more like real bears than teddy bears. In 1902 Margarete's nephew designed a more friendly-looking bear with movable joints. It is now widely believed that this was the world's first teddy bear — although it was to be some years before the name teddy bear was used for this new toy.

Early Steiff bears are now extremely collectable and command high prices, especially those that are in good condition. Made from quality mohair and stuffed with wood wool (also known as excelsior), they typically have long shaved muzzles and pronounced humps on their backs. Their arms are long and curve upwards at the paws, and they have relatively long legs with shapely ankles and large feet.

To distinguish their bears from those of other manufacturers, Steiff introduced their famous Button in Ear trademark in 1904 and patented it in 1905. From then on, all Steiff toys carried a button in their left ear.

In 1996 a survey discovered that more than 98% of German households owned an animal soft toy, and of these 88% were made by Steiff.

Steiff have designed more than 15,000 toys since 1880, and around 200 new ones are introduced each year. There are about 800 in the current range alone. In all, approximately one and a half million toys leave the factory each year, and of these some 350,000

(70%) are bears. In 1992 a Steiff Collectors Club was set up. Within five years it boasted a membership of more than 25,000.

In 1980 Steiff celebrated 100 years of toy making by introducing its very first limited-edition bear for collectors. Papa Bear was a replica of a traditional mohair fully jointed teddy, first made in 1903. The new bear was limited to 11,000 world-wide; 5,000 had certificates in English and were intended for the US market.

Many other Steiff collectors' bears have followed — some of them using early patterns and others new designs. Among them are bears for sale only in one country, or made exclusively for a single shop. A few have been limited to just hundreds, but most to a few thousand. These are keenly sought by collectors, and values can increase rapidly once the complete edition has been sold.

Although Steiff is the most famous of all the German soft toy companies, bears made by several other German manufacturers are also highly collectable. Nuremberg's Gebrüder Bing, for instance, made many beautiful bears from about 1907 onward.

Early Bing bears were very like those made by Steiff. They also made mechanical bears, which are especially popular today. In addition to somersaulting bears, there were walking bears, bears on roller skates and a footballing bear with a clockwork mechanism inside the ball to make it turn.

The German company Schreyer & Co. (tradename Schuco) produced a whole range of miniature bears that were intended to be carried in ladies' handbags or kept on the dressing table. Made in a variety of colours, they included a bear whose head could be removed to reveal a tiny perfume bottle, and a bear containing a powder compact, mirror and lipstick. Another little bear squirted perfume through a small hole in his nose when his body was squeezed.

Schuco also made tiny tumbling bears, and miniature 'Roller Teddies' in little wooden cars. There was also the 'two-faced' Janus: twisting a knob at the base of his body transformed his face from benign and smiling to wicked, with staring eyes and tongue poking out. Best known of all were the little Yes/No bears. When their tails were moved up and down or from side to side, they nodded or shook their heads.

Many early German bear manufacturers were based in and around the town of Sonneberg in Thüringia. Although most have today been forgotten, the companies formed by members of the Hermann family became known all over the world, and two are still in business today.

Johann Hermann was the first of the family to set up his own toy-making workshop. Very much a family concern, all six of his children — three sons and three daughters — worked with him before his sons went on to set up companies of their own.

In 1911, Bernhard Hermann was the first of the three Hermann brothers to set up his own bear-making business. In his factory he made high quality mohair bears under the name BEHA (a phonetic spelling of his initials). He also used homeworkers to make a cheaper range. Most of the better bears were sold to customers in America, Canada and England, and some went to Swiss department stores. Many were made from short mohair, with an inset muzzle of a lighter colour in clipped plush. He also made cheaper bears, but these remained in Germany, where they were offered as prizes in amusement parks and lotteries.

Bernhard's four sons all worked for their father in due course. After the war Sonneberg became part of East Germany and in 1948 the factory moved to the American Zone. Today the company is known as Teddy-Hermann, reflecting the continued importance of teddy bears in its production.

Like his brother Bernhard, Max Hermann also set up a business of his own. He had worked with his father for some years, and following his father's death, formed his own company in the toy-making town of Sonneberg in 1920. After the Second World War the firm (now in East Germany) was gradually taken over by the state. Early in 1953, Max and his family escaped to the West, where they had already set up a subsidiary. There the company thrived. It is still in business today, making toys under the name Hermann-Spielwaren — including some bears made especially for the collectors' market.

The Ideal Novelty and Toy Company was founded by Rose and Morris Michtom in New York in 1903. They had been inspired to make their very first bear after seeing the now-famous Clifford Berryman cartoon depicting President Roosevelt's refusal to shoot a captive bear. Whether theirs was the very first teddy bear in the world is a matter for continued debate; the success of their company, however, is beyond dispute, as it rapidly expanded to become a huge corporation with a vast turnover, making a wide range of toys.

Early Ideal bears weren't labelled, so they can be difficult to identify, typical characteristics include wide, very triangular heads and rather long bodies. The mohair tends to have a short pile, and the stuffing is wood wool, which feels crunchy when squeezed.

Many American bear-making companies were only in business for a relatively short time, and their bears are now extremely rare and much sought after by collectors, especially if complete with an identifying label. More enduring was the Knickerbocker Toy

Company, set up in Albany, New York, in 1869, making educational toys. The first Knickerbocker teddy bears and other soft toys appeared in the 1920s. Today, early Knickerbocker bears, with their broad heads and shaved muzzles, are very popular with collectors. Later bears often had unusual 'spangle' eyes, with black lines radiating out from the pupils.

After the Second World War, factories in the Far East began mass-producing inexpensive teddy bears and other soft toys, to be exported all over the world. A number of American companies, both old and new, responded to this competition by designing their own bears as usual but having some or all made in the Far East to keep prices down. Wholly American-made bears became few and far between.

Some of the first, and best, British bears were made by the London company J.K. Farnell, who numbered prestigious London department store Harrods amongst its customers. The bear bought there by A.A. Milne's wife in 1921 is thought to have been made by Farnell. He was a gift for her son Christopher Robin and was later to provide the inspiration for *Winnie-the-Pooh*.

Pooh now lives in the Children's Room of the New York Public Library on West 53rd Street — along with his friends Piglet, Eeyore, Tigger and Kanga. They had toured the US in 1947 and never returned home.

B ritain's oldest surviving manufacturer of teddy bears is Dean's, set up by Boer War Veteran Henry Samuel Dean in 1902. At first, the company made only rag books designed for children who 'wear their food and eat their clothes'. An early addition to the company's range were their Knockabout Toy Sheets — cloth sheets which were printed with all the pieces needed to make a soft toy. One of these featured a bear. Instructions for making up the toy were also included and the final result was, like the rag books, able to withstand a great deal of wear and tear.

Dean's made their first teddy bears during the First World War, but it was in the 1920s that they started making bears in significant numbers. Even then, they were better-known for dolls than bears. Today, Dean's are based in Wales and alongside their children's toys they now make bears specially for collectors. Some of these are replicas of early Dean's bears, others are new designs — among them a whole series of bears designed by leading bear artists from various countries.

One of the most famous of all the British soft toy companies was Chad Valley, whose first teddy bears appeared during the First World War.

The company, whose range included everything from metal toys to jigsaw puzzles and dolls, expanded enormously between the wars, opening new factories to cope with the demand. Many different bears were introduced, including novelties like clowns and bears in vivid colours.

During the 1970s recession, however, the Chad Valley factories started to close, and by 1980 all had gone. Now the Chad Valley name is owned by the Woolworth's store chain.

In 1938, Britain's Chad Valley Company was granted a Royal Warrant of Appointment. They proudly recorded this information on their labels, and this now helps collectors to date some Chad Valley bears. At first the labels declared that the company were 'Toy Makers to Her Majesty the Queen', the Queen in question being the wife of George VI, now the Queen Mother. After the coronation of Queen Elizabeth II in 1953, the wording became 'Toy Makers to H.M. Queen Elizabeth the Queen Mother'.

Among the best-loved of all British bears are those carrying the name Chiltern. Perhaps the most widely collected are the Hugmee range, which were first seen in 1923. There were many different Hugmee designs — so many, in fact, that some enthusiasts have built their whole collection around these bears.

Chunky thighs, often likened to chicken drumsticks, and long arms were among the characteristics of the earliest Hugmees. They also had long muzzles which, during the 1930s, were usually shaved. After the Second World War, faces became flatter, limbs became shorter and feet smaller.

In 1930 a new soft toy company, Merrythought Ltd, was set up in Coalbrookdale, Shropshire, by two Yorkshire mohair spinners concerned that their mohair was no longer in demand for clothing and furnishings. Within months the trade press was referring to the company's splendid range and high quality. Merrythought has remained one of Britain's leading soft toy manufacturers ever since.

One of the first directors of Merrythought had been the head of production at nearby Chad Valley. He brought with him several skilled Chad Valley employees, including the talented designer Florence Atwood, who all helped to ensure the company's rapid success.

Teddy bears were included in their very first catalogue and have been in the range ever since. Today, early Merrythought bears are highly collectable; the company also makes many special collectors' editions, with a large number of new designs introduced each year and sold all over the world.

B y the 1950s, safety and hygiene were the big selling points for all kinds of toys and teddy bears were no exception. The British firm Wendy Boston was a leading player in this field: their greatest innovation was the locked-in safety eye. This fixed into the bear's head with a nut, washer and bolt, and once attached was virtually impossible to remove.

In 1954 they launched fully washable bears — foam-filled,

unjointed and with nylon fur. A leading washing machine manufacturer tested them and awarded a 'Certificate of Washability',
which confirmed that they could withstand four minutes in a spin
dryer! Adverts even showed a hapless waterlogged bear being run
through a mangle without apparent damage.

A number of other manufacturers also made washable bears
— some of which were fully jointed.

In the early years of this century, many mechanical toys — including bears — were produced by French manufacturers. Fernand Martin made a fierce-looking bear with metal feet that shuffled awkwardly along and in 1911 the Paris-based firm of Pintel made a tumbling clown bear. It was only after the First World War that the French soft toy industry really came into its own, and large numbers of teddy bears were made.

Marcel Pintel was amongst the best-known French teddy bear manufacturers, although other successful French companies set up between the wars included FADAP (Fabrication Artistique d'Animaux en Peluche), ALFA (Article de Luxe Fabrication Artisanale), and the company set up by Emile Thiennot.

In the 1950s the French teddy bear industry enjoyed its greatest boom and many new manufacturers appeared. By the 1960s, however, many of these companies were already in decline and by the 1980s most French teddy bear manufacturers had disappeared.

Teddy bears enjoyed early popularity in Australia, but although soft toy koalas were made there, it seems that the only teddy bears that were on sale were imported ones, most having been made in Britain. Only after the First World War, when Australians began insisting on more Australian-made goods, did the country's own teddy bear industry come into being. The first of the makers was Joy Toys, with Emil, Berlex and Lindee among those which followed.

A characteristic of Australian bears is that by the 1930s most were made with unjointed, stiff necks — possibly a cost-cutting exercise. Apart from this they had much in common with British bears of the time. Many, however, had extra long stitches on either side of the nose, usually protruding upwards and often giving them a distinctly glum expression.

M any of the bears bought by today's collectors are made not by manufacturers but by teddy bear 'artists', who design and sew bears in their own homes or small workshops. Most sew every stitch themselves, but some enlist help, often from family members, to help with the more routine tasks.

Designs range from simple traditional bears, adorned with nothing more elaborate than a bow, to exquisitely dressed and accessorised creations that sell for vast sums. The most elaborate bears are usually totally unique 'one-offs', which increases their appeal to collectors. Others are made in limited editions — often as small as three or four, although occasionally consisting of 100 or more bears. A few artists also make unlimited 'open' editions.

M ost bear lovers who enjoy sewing or other crafts decide at some stage to try making a bear themselves. Some stop after just one or two, having satisfied their curiosity; others enjoy it so much that what started as a hobby turns into a full-time occupation — designing and making bears to sell to shops or at teddy bear fairs.

These teddy bear artists, first seen in the US, soon began to appear in other countries where teddy bears are collected. In Britain, for instance, an abundance of bear-making courses (initially led by American artists) has helped the number of artists to multiply from a handful to many hundred in just a few years. In the Netherlands, where sewing of all kinds is hugely popular, a large number of bear lovers make bears as well as collecting them.

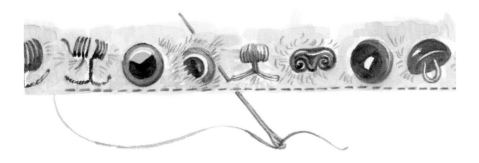

Most bear artists develop their own distinctive style. Perhaps all their bears have certain facial characteristics in common — a particular muzzle shape, or perhaps a distinctive form of nose stitching. They may make pretty bears or glum bears, or show particular flair when dressing or accessorising their creations.

Artists in Australia often produce highly innovative designs on account of their distance from the influence of other artists. Early Japanese artists made inventive use of a variety of fabrics, since mohair fur was not readily available, and some South African makers have created distinctive bears using locally woven mohair — very different from cloths made in other countries.

CHAPTER THREE

famous bears

No one has yet come up with any single reason why teddy bears have such wide appeal. From childhood on teddies are friends and comforters, but while many other soft toys are cheerfully abandoned, teddy-love often endures into adulthood and even old age. Nor is it restricted to one section of society, or even one country. Bear lovers are everywhere — even amongst the rich and famous, and sometimes it is the bears themselves that make their owners rich and famous!

The first famous fictional bears were the Roosevelt Bears, Teddy B and Teddy G — the B and G standing for black and grey, not bad and good as many people believe. In spite of their names, the bears looked much more like real bears than teddies, although they tended to act very like teddies whenever children were around.

Their creator Seymour Eaton wasn't at all sure how well his stories would be received, and hid behind the pseudonym Paul Piper when they first appeared in American newspapers early in 1906. But readers loved them, and he quickly reverted to his real name. The stories were gathered together in a number of books, and the bears began to appear on postcards, writing paper and china as their popularity grew.

One of the most enduring of all fictional bears is Rupert, who lives in Nutwood with his friends — Bill Badger, Algy Pug, Edward Trunk and Podgy Pig. In many ways, he's more like a little boy than a bear. In fact, it's been said that parents like him because he's the ideal son: kind, considerate, well-mannered, intelligent — and he never seems to get dirty!

Rupert was created by British artist and illustrator Mary Tourtel. Her husband was night editor of the *Daily Express*, which wanted a character that could compete with Teddy Tail, who appeared in a rival newspaper.

The first Rupert story, told in rhyming couplets, appeared on 8th November 1920, tucked away on the paper's women's page. The little bear, however, soon found popularity with a far wider readership, a popularity that continues today.

Mary Tourtel drew all the stories herself until in 1935 failing eyesight forced her to give up. She was succeeded by Alfred Bestall, who was responsible for the first of the now-famous Rupert annuals, which appeared in 1936. Bestall continued to draw the newspaper stories for 30 years (and the covers of the annual covers for even longer), before he in turn handed the little bear over to a new generation.

The earliest Rupert annuals in mint condition now command high prices, but more recent publications are far more affordable — especially secondhand copies in less than pristine condition. Rupert has also appeared on a wide range of other merchandise, ranging from Easter eggs and children's clothing to china, lamps and clocks.

Rupert is usually drawn with white fur, except on the covers of the Rupert annuals, where his fur is brown. In Dutch he is still known as Bruintje Beer, or Brown Bear.

P robably the most famous bear of all, and certainly one of the best-loved, is Winnie-the-Pooh. Originally called Edward Bear, his picture was first seen illustrating a poem called 'Teddy Bear', published in Punch on 13th February 1924. The drawing was by E.H. Shepard, and the poem was the work of a successful playwright and novelist by the name of A.A. Milne.

Later that year, a number of Milne's verses were collected together in a book called *When We Were Very Young*, and Edward Bear appeared there too. He was so popular that two years later he was given a new name and a whole book of his own — *Winnie-the-Pooh*. A second book, *The House at Pooh Corner*, followed.

Winnie-the-Pooh has remained a favourite with both children and adults ever since. Pooh's original owner, Christopher Robin Milne, attributed the success of the books to the fact that they were meant to be read aloud — A.A. Milne actually dictated the stories to his wife, who typed them, so that he could gauge the reaction of his audience.

MUCH CREDIT FOR THE SUCCESS OF WINNIE-THE-POOH HAS BEEN GIVEN TO E.H. SHEPARD'S DRAWINGS, WHICH FITTED THE TEXT SO WELL. HIS DRAWINGS, HOWEVER, WEREN'T BASED ON POOH HIMSELF BUT ON A BEAR CALLED GROWLER OWNED BY SHEPARD'S SON, GRAHAM.

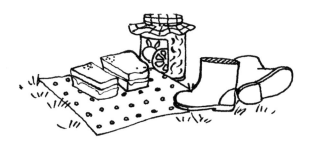

Forty years ago, writer Michael Bond sat at his typewriter wondering how to fill the blank sheet of paper in front of him. Then he started to write about the little bear he'd bought his wife for Christmas, and ten days later he had written a whole book. The bear was called Paddington, because the couple lived near Paddington Station in London at the time, and the book was *A Bear Called Paddington*, published in 1958.

The accident-prone bear from darkest Peru was an immediate success in his duffel coat and battered old hat (which

often had one of his favourite marmalade sandwiches concealed beneath it). His famous Wellingtons came later: they
were added by Shirley Clarkson, who created the first
Paddington soft toys (in 1972) and simply wanted the bears to
stand up! The soft toys also carry a luggage label with the
words 'Please look after this bear' — as worn by Paddington in
the first of the books, when he was discovered on Paddington
Station.

More Paddington books followed, with over twenty million copies sold all over the world. Paddington has starred in
his own BBC television series, which used Paddington puppets, and more recently in a series of cartoons. The little bear
has also appeared on clothing, soft furnishings, games and
foods — including, of course, marmalade.

A rather worn teddy bear found unexpected fame when he was given a starring role in the televised adaptation of Evelyn Waugh's *Brideshead Revisited*. The bear's name was Delicatessen, but he will forever be associated with the character he played in the series — Aloysius, the constant companion of Lord Sebastian Flyte. Waugh based Flyte's love of bears on that of John Betjeman, who took his own bear, Archie, to university with him.

Delicatessen was owned by British actor and bear lover Peter Bull, who had received him as a gift from the owner of a 'dried goods store' in Maine. The bear (by then aged 62) had sat in the store for 55 years, and seemed destined for a long and quiet retirement in England, but his acting debut changed all that. When Brideshead star Anthony Andrews went to America to promote the series there, Delicatessen went too — leaving his pawprint outside Grauman's Chinese Theatre while he was there. He made many public appearances together with Peter Bull, and it was rumoured that he once disappeared to Venice with Lord Olivier. After Peter's death in 1984, Delicatessen lived in the US for a while. He is now resident at 'Teddy Bears' of Witney in Oxfordshire.

John Betjeman, Britain's Poet Laureate from 1972 to 1984, had a much-loved teddy bear called Archie (or, to give him his complete name, Archibald Ormsby Gore). Betjeman took the bear up to Oxford with him and later immortalised him in the famous auto-biographical poem 'Summoned by Bells', which was published in 1960. The bear appeared again in the short poem 'Archibald', and later in the delightful story of *Archie & the Strict Baptists*, which told some of his youthful adventures.

YOGI BEAR IS SAID TO HAVE TAKEN HIS NAME FROM THAT OF THE US BASEBALL PLAYER YOGI BERRA. THE BEAR WAS FIRST SEEN IN THE 1960S, IN A SERIES OF TELEVISION CARTOONS AND IN A 1964 FEATURE FILM. SINCE THEN A NUMBER OF COMPANIES HAVE MADE YOGI SOFT TOYS, THERE HAVE BEEN SOFT TOY VERSIONS OF HIS LITTLE FRIEND BOO BOO AND EVEN OF HIS OFTEN-FORGOTTEN GIRLFRIEND CINDY, WHO ONLY MADE OCCASIONAL APPEARANCES IN THE SHOWS. BRITISH SOFT TOY COMPANY MERRYTHOUGHT MADE GIANT YOGI NIGHTDRESS CASES. THERE HAVE BEEN YOGI BEARS WITH VINYL FACES, AS WELL AS YOGIS MADE ENTIRELY OF PLASTIC, NOT TO MENTION BOOKS, COMICS AND A VARIETY OF OTHER ITEMS.

One of the first bears to find fame on the TV screen was a glove puppet called Sooty. He was spotted by an electrical engineer called Harry Corbett during a holiday in Blackpool in 1948.

Corbett was an entertainer in his spare time and the bear soon joined him on stage — his golden ears blackened with soot, giving him a more distinctive appearance as well as a new name. By the early 1950s he was making regular television appearances and soon had his own TV series. A dog called Sweep joined him, and then a panda called Soo — despite initial objections from the BBC that she would introduce a totally unacceptable sexual element!

Harry's son Matthew later took over from his father, and the little bear has remained as popular as ever. Each year there is a vast turnover from the sale of merchandise featuring Sooty and his friends, with everything from stationery and balloons to watches and money boxes. Enduring favourites are the glove puppets themselves, made for many years by Britain's Chad Valley company, but now produced in the Far East.

For many years, one of the residents at a Lancashire museum was a little bear reputed to have survived the sinking of the Titanic in 1912.

Vittorio Gatti had given the much-loved teddy bear to his father Gaspare, when he joined the fated ship as catering manager. Gaspare Gatti never returned, but the bear was apparently found tucked safely in his tobacco pouch and was returned to his widow Edith. When Edith died, 50 years later, the little bear finally came back to Vittorio himself, who loved to tell the Titanic Bear's story to his grandchildren and great-grandchildren.

After Vittorio Gatti's death, the little bear took up residence in a Lancashire museum. In 1992 the British soft toy manufacturer Merrythought produced their own (slightly larger) version in a limited edition of 5,000 — exactly 80 years after the sinking of the Titanic. The original bear is now in a private collection.

In May 1912, Steiff were asked to make several hundred black bears to send to Britain, which was in mourning following the sinking of the Titanic. Only 494 bears were made and they sold quickly. They now fetch huge sums at auction if in good condition.

British actor Peter Bull became as famous for his love of bears as for his film roles. He was often asked to talk about bears on television and radio programmes on both sides of the Atlantic, and was invariably accompanied by a little bear called Theodore, who usually travelled in Peter's top pocket. Peter used to call him a symbol of unloneliness. If Theodore was with him, even the emptiest of hotel rooms would still feel like home.

After Peter's death, little Theodore lived for many years with Peter's friend Enid Irving. He can now be found at 'Teddy Bears' of Witney in Oxfordshire, together with another of Peter's much-loved bears, Delicatessen.

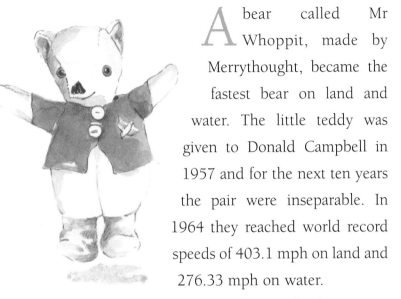

A bear called Mr Whoppit, made by Merrythought, became the fastest bear on land and water. The little teddy was given to Donald Campbell in 1957 and for the next ten years the pair were inseparable. In 1964 they reached world record speeds of 403.1 mph on land and 276.33 mph on water.

The bear also managed to survive the fastest ever automobile crash, but lost both his feet in another horrifying accident. In 1967, Campbell's boat sank during a further world record attempt. Campbell himself was never found, but the little bear floated to the surface and was rescued.

In May 1989, a bright red bear made by the German company Steiff broke the existing world record price for a teddy bear when he sold for £12,100 at Christie's in London's South Kensington. His colour made him an extremely rare bear, but it was his story that really captured the public's imagination. The little red bear called Alfonzo had once belonged to a Russian princess. He had been a gift from George Mikhailovich, Grand Duke of Russia, to his daughter Princess Xenia. The Grand Duke was assassinated in 1919, but the bear remained with his daughter for the rest of her life.

Many of the bear's early years had been spent in the Crimea, close to the residence of the Tsar himself. He may also have visited the princess's grandfather, whose father was Tsar Nicholas I.

Alfonzo is now the star of the museum at the Oxfordshire shop 'Teddy Bears' of Witney, but occasionally he makes guest appearances at major teddy bear exhibitions in other parts of the world.

When American Paul Volpp decided to buy a bear as a 42nd anniversary present for his wife Rosemary in 1989, he never suspected that his private gesture of love would become world news. The bear was a beautiful Steiff in unusual brown-tipped mohair and Paul was not the only one determined to buy her.

When the hammer finally fell, Paul was £55,000 poorer.

The bear was christened Happy Anniversary (or Happy for short) and went on to raise large sums for various charities through personal appearances all over the world.

The world record price for a teddy bear is currently £110,000 — paid at Christie's in London in December 1994 for a beautiful cinnamon-coloured Steiff called Teddy Girl. She had been the lifelong companion of Colonel T.R. Henderson, and for many years was known as Teddy Boy until one night she turned up for dinner in a dress and was promptly renamed!

Colonel Bob, as he was affectionately known, was founder of the UK branch of Good Bears of the World — an organisation set up to provide teddy bears for children and adults in need of comfort. A much-loved figure in the teddy bear world, he was often seen with Teddy Girl at events for bear lovers, and their pictures appeared in several early books about bear collecting.

Even without such a history, Teddy Girl would have been special. Her cinnamon fur and the centre seam in her head are both rare, but it was her background that ensured her place in teddy bear history. Bought by Yoshihiro Sekiguchi, a Japanese toy manufacturer, she is now the star attraction in his museum near Tokyo.

One of the world's most-travelled bears is Teddy Edward, star of many books by photographer Patrick Matthews and his wife Mollie. Patrick photographed Teddy Edward on Mount Everest, in Timbuktu, and in many other parts of the world while working on photographic assignments. When he returned home, Mollie added the words. Later, some of the pictures were turned into a series of 13 films for BBC television.

In 1996, Teddy Edward was sold at Christie's along with some of the props used in the photos — among them his little helicopter, jeep, bicycle and castle. His new owner is Japanese toy manufacturer and museum owner Yoshihiro Sekiguchi, who had paid a word record price for Teddy Girl two years earlier.

M any well-loved childhood teddies have seen their owners go on to find fame and fortune. A bear called Humphrey, for instance, was photographed outside his home at 10 Downing Street when Margaret Thatcher was Britain's Prime Minister. The Iron Lady was not at all embarrassed to admit that he had been with her since childhood.

Other bears have been given to stars of stage and screen by fans. Bear-loving Elvis Presley received thousands after the release of 'Teddy Bear' in 1957, while Paul McCartney's love of Rupert led to him producing the award-winning short, 'Rupert and the Frog Song'. Another former Beatle, Ringo Starr, owns a much-loved giant panda known as Chairman of the Board.

A little bear called Mishka has been a popular character in Russian folklore for centuries. More recently, he became the hero of a cartoon series in which his adventures even included space travel like that of the Russian astronauts. In 1980 he became the mascot for the Moscow Olympics — but with the more 'international' name of Misha.

Soft toy versions of the bear, complete with belt showing the Olympic rings, were made in many countries. A large number of metal souvenir badges were also produced — some showing the little bear participating in various Olympic sports. Plastic Mishas and many other Misha souvenirs were sold and are now being sought by collectors.

Bears have been used to promote products as diverse as sand-paper and chocolate — often with overwhelming success. A bear given to new account holders at an American bank proved so popular that the offer had to be withdrawn when existing customers started to close their accounts and open new ones just to acquire the bear!

The British company Bear Brand used a bear to advertise their hosiery. At first, in the 1920s, he was a rather fearsome-looking real bear, but by the 1940s he had evolved into a more cuddly teddy bear. Later, giant Chad Valley bears were used in Bear Brand shop displays.

More recently, Celestial Seasons in the US depicted a sleeping bear on their Sleepytime® herb tea. He proved so popular that they adopted the little bear as their company logo. Special Sleepybears are sold in the factory shop, and he has also appeared on clocks, mugs, tea pots, aprons, T-shirts, caps, book bags and various other exclusive Sleepytime® items.

bear collecting

M ost dealers in bears old and new offer the same advice: collectors should only buy bears that they really love. A bear that is bought purely for its monetary value and possible investment potential will never give as much pleasure as one bought simply for its appeal. This is an important point to remember when faced with an overwhelming choice at a teddy bear fair or in a teddy bear shop.

Bear lovers haven't always had so large a choice of bears and bear-related products. Just a few years ago, many simply bought anything to do with bears that they saw — there were so few to be found. It was easy enough to find mass-produced teddies made in the Far East, but traditional jointed bears made from high quality fabrics like mohair were rare. Most were still languishing in sheds and attics – packed away and forgotten by their original owners.

A bear loved since childhood will often be priceless to his owner — even with all his fur hugged off and perhaps an ear long lost. Some collectors, too, like well-worn teds. There's a feeling that they've a real story to tell — if only they were able. But it's bears who've never been loved, who've sat unwanted on a shelf or who've been brought out only on high days and holidays, with their fur still pristine and just like new, who usually fetch the highest prices.

I n general, rare bears are more sought after than mass-produced ones, but it needs to be a kind of rarity that is in demand. A 'one-off' bear by a novice maker will be totally unique, and yet it will only sell for a fraction of the price of most older bears.

With older bears, the make is important: those made by companies renowned for their high quality and good design will always be most sought after. If only a limited number of a design were made, this also helps boost the price, as will an interesting and well-documented history. A well-loved bear once owned by royalty, for instance, could fetch more than a pristine cousin. It always pays to find out as much as possible about a bear's history, or provenance — and it's even better if you can obtain pictures of him taken with his original owner when he was still just a cub!

Finally, an appealing face will also increase the bear's selling power. It's not something that can be defined — a mouth of a certain shape or eyes placed just so. It's often called simply the 'Aaaah factor'.

E arly bears can be very valuable, especially if they are known to be the work of a good manufacturer. Those by the German company Steiff routinely fetch high prices — up to thousands of pounds for the rarest bears, such as those in more unusual colours like white, black or cinnamon. Early bears by other leading German companies like Bing are also keenly collected.

The oldest bears by top British and American companies like Farnell and Ideal can also be well beyond the means of the average collector, but more recent 'oldies' are often more affordable — especially if the bears have been well cuddled in their youth. In Britain, for instance, collectors continue to find interesting bears by companies like Chad Valley, Merrythought, Chiltern and Pedigree turning up at markets and in charity shops, but as more and more people become aware of the value of older teds, bargains become harder to find. Modern bears manufactured specifically for collectors are now widely available in department stores, gift shops and toy shops. German companies like Steiff and Hermann introduce new collectors' ranges each year, as do British companies such as Merrythought and Dean's.

Some of these bears are exact replicas of earlier designs. Others may be totally new — sometimes dressed and accessorised to give them extra character. Sporting bears, painters, chefs and musicians are just a few of those created to date and sold all over the world.

For decades, bears were sold only in toy shops and in the toy departments of larger stores, but in recent years specialist bear shops have opened in many countries. Most sell a wide range of new bears both manufactured and artist-made. A few sell old bears too. They often have a selection of bear-related items, which can range from inexpensive teddy fridge magnets and postcards to beautifully crafted bear-sized furniture.

Visits to teddy bear fairs are often important fixtures on the bear lover's calendar, and are an excellent place for both the novice and the experienced collector to add to their family of bears.

Events large and small are held in many countries, with some bear lovers travelling vast distances to attend major events. The smallest fairs often consist of just a handful of stalls and attract relatively few visitors. The largest events offer collectors an overwhelming choice, with hundreds of artists, shops, dealers in old bears and sellers of all manner of bear-related items taking stands. Sometimes a fair will be part of a whole teddy bear convention with informative talks and perhaps even bear-making workshops.

Since the early 1980s, teddy bears have been going under the hammer in toy sales at a number of London auction houses. Special teddy bear auctions have also been held in many other countries where bears are collected. Often these are included as part of teddy bear conventions and other events, or are sometimes used as a way of raising money for good causes. Christie's in London's South Kensington holds a special all-teddy sale each December, attended by collectors from all over the world.

Many bear lovers are nervous about attending auctions, afraid that if they blow their noses they might unwittingly place a bid! Although the pace of an auction can seem a little daunting at first, making a bid need not be frightening. Attending auctions can be fascinating, even for those not intending to buy.

The bears will be on view for some time before the sale — on preceding days, or earlier on the day of the auction itself. Viewings can be a splendid place to see and learn about old bears. Even the rarest and most valuable can usually be inspected closely — and cuddled! Not many museums allow that. A catalogue will give a description of the lots and often includes estimated selling prices, although it's best to inspect bears closely before deciding whether to bid. It's also advisable to enquire about methods of payment, as storage or carriage charges may be made for purchases not immediately paid for and collected.

Above all, decide in advance the maximum price you are willing to pay (remembering additional costs like the buyer's premium). This will help you to avoid being carried away in the heat of the moment. An auctioneer's job is to obtain the highest price possible, and some are very adept at persuading hesitaters to go just one bid further.

Postal or telephone bids can often be placed in advance by those unable to attend the sale. If you attend in person you'll usually be asked to register beforehand, you will then be given a numbered card or paddle to wave in the air to place your bids.

Finally, if you decide to have a go yourself, arrive in plenty of time. Once the sale starts, bidding can be fast and furious — many a novice has missed a coveted bear by arriving too late!

A good way to gather a fascinating, if not necessarily valuable, collection on a budget is to choose a single theme. A large group of bears sold as football club mascots, for example, could be quite a talking point, while a couple of more collectable teds costing a similar sum might hardly be noticed.

A little ingenuity can turn just one or two bears into a whole collection — without breaking the bank. The trick is to look out for related items to display with the bears. A very ordinary bear will look much more impressive if a postcard or greetings card showing a similar bear is put on show with him. Modern manufactured bears could be put together with company catalogues or even a framed magazine article in which they are featured. Bears promoting a certain product become much more interesting if displayed with some advertisements for the same commodity.

Simple props bought inexpensively at flea markets and junk shops can make all the difference to the impact of a collection. Bears can look good seated in child-sized chairs, grouped together in cots and prams, perched on rocking horses or on the backs of wheeled animals, and tucked into children's cars or other vehicles. Old toys and books often go well with older bears. Modern toys made from traditional materials like wood may make suitable playthings for younger teds. Tiny baskets and straw hats can sometimes be picked up for next to nothing, and doll's house furniture can often be used to good effect with miniature bears.

Collectors and bear makers often disagree about whether bears should be dressed or left 'in the fur'. Some find even a simple bow excessive, whereas others will search long and hard to find just the right outfit for a favourite ted.

Old bears often look splendid in antique doll's clothes or children's wear found at antique fairs and fleamarkets or specialist doll fairs. Bears tend to have large heads, thick necks, round tums and chubby arms, all of which must be taken into account when buying clothes for them! Sometimes a simple lace collar or shawl can be the answer to the problem.

Charity shops and street markets are often a good source of inexpensive outfits for newer bears. Clothes made specifically for bears can also sometimes be found at bear fairs and in specialist shops, and so can patterns for teddy-sized clothing. Lovely new clothes for old bears can often be cut from tattered garments bought cheaply at flea markets. That lovely old fabric might be full of holes, but it could just contain enough good pieces to make a beautiful new jacket for a well-loved old bear!

Teddy bear postcards began to appear soon after the first teddy bears, and thousands have been published over the years. Some of the most collectable are those which are drawn by well-known artists of their time, like Lawson Wood, Donald McGill and William Henry Ellam.

Early photographic 'portrait' cards are also of special interest to lovers of old bears, although serious postcard collectors may say that these are not really postcards at all. They are simply studio photographs with postcard-style printing on the back. Their attraction is that they often show beautiful early teddy bears — many photographers kept a teddy in their studio to use as a prop when photographing children. Doting parents would send copies of the picture to family and friends, simply scribbling an address and short message on the reverse.

Many of the deckle-edged cards popular in the 1930s included photographs of bears — often together with a suitable birthday or anniversary rhyme. There are dozens of inexpensive modern postcards to collect, too. Some show photos of bears old and new, while others, often humorous, are drawn by artists of today. Some reprints of earlier cards have also appeared.

As with bears themselves, specialising can add extra impact to collections of bear-related items. Even a small collection of teddy bear china or games, of silver or pewter items, or of carved wooden bears can be quite a talking point if displayed together.

Some of the most interesting postcard collections are created by specialising in a single theme. The subject may be quite broad — early artist-drawn cards, for example, or it could be much more specific, like sporting bears or bears of a particular make. Whole collections can also be built around birthday or Christmas postcards, or cards showing particular bears such as Winnie-the-Pooh or Rupert.

Even before the first teddy was made, real bears were adorning all manner of useful and decorative items. Carved wooden bears, for instance, were incorporated into smokers' requisites like ash-trays, pipe holders and matchbox containers. Bears held ink wells or pens, and were turned into clothes brushes or larger items like hat stands. These wooden animals used to be called Black Forest bears although it is now known that many were made in Switzerland and Russia.

It would be possible to decorate virtually a whole house with furnishings and ornaments featuring teddy bears. They are available adorning wallpaper and wallpaper borders, curtains, bed linen, lamps, clocks, china, cutlery, towels, rugs, cushions, oven gloves, soap dishes, toothbrushes — even shower curtains, ironing board covers and draught excluders! Bears have been painted on cupboards, bed heads, chairs and benches; they decorate pens and pencils, writing paper, bookends and toy boxes. There are tiny mass-produced figurines and giant porcelain teds made in exclusive limited editions. If a bear lover can think of it, the chances are that someone has made it for them to collect.

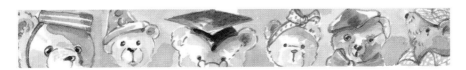

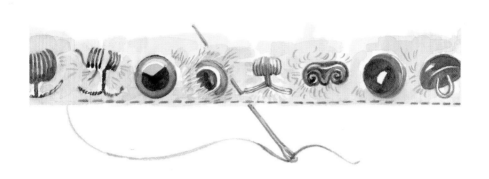

bear making & maintenance

The earliest teddy bears were made from mohair, which took its name from an Arabic word meaning 'cloth of bright goat's hair'. The goats in question are Angora goats, once found mainly in the Angora or Ankara region of Turkey but today also bred in a handful of other countries, including South Africa.

Yorkshire became the great mohair spinning and weaving centre — the woven mohair was sometimes called 'Yorkshire cloth'. Today much mohair cloth is woven in Germany.

Mohair yarn is soft and silky and the woven plush can be given many different finishes. There are short-pile furs which feel bristly, and fabrics with a luxurious long pile which can be curled or waved; sometimes the pile is 'distressed' to give it an older look. Dozens of colours are now on sale, including 'tipped' furs, where a second colour is brushed across the tips of the pile. Many teddy bear artists are also now experimenting with dyes, sometimes even hand-painting the fabric to achieve a particular look.

M any fabrics have been turned into teddy bears over the years. Traditional mohair may be mixed with wool or cotton, for instance, or even with silk to give it a wonderfully luxurious feel. Alpaca wool has also been used for teddy bears, as has cotton plush, which is much less expensive than mohair.

Many furs have been created from man-made fibres, especially since the Second World War. Art silk, or artificial silk, was used for many British bears from the late 1920s until its high flammability resulted in it falling foul of safety regulations. After the war, synthetic acrylic furs were widely used.

Home-made bears are found in an even wider variety of fabrics – from towelling and blankets to printed cottons and curtaining.

W ool felt was used for the foot and paw pads of most early bears, although sometimes a woven cloth similar to cotton was used. A kind of oil cloth known as Rexine is found on the pads of some British bears from the 1940s and 50s. Now both man-ufacturers and artists use a wide range of natural and synthetic fabrics, including leather, suede, suedette, velveteen, cor-duroy, cotton and various kinds of plush. Sometimes claws are added — hand-stitched as a finishing touch.

Most traditional bears have heads and limbs that move with the help of 'joints'. At first, these were made from cardboard discs, held together by a metal pin. The cardboard was later replaced by longer-lasting hardboard and metal washers were used as reinforcement, to prevent the pin from tearing the discs. Even today, manufacturers of traditional bears — especially those intended for collectors — often use these 'cotter pin' joints, as do many artists. Some artists, however, prefer a new version in which the cotter pins are replaced by nuts and bolts.

A more recent introduction is the plastic safety joint, in which one disc is made with a shank onto which a smaller disc can be clipped. Once fixed together, these discs are virtually impossible to separate. They are widely used in teddies intended for children, which must satisfy stringent safety regulations.

Before the First World War, most teddy bear eyes were made from wooden boot buttons, usually coloured black. Glass eyes later began to replace them — especially from the 1920s onwards. Some were made of clear glass, which was painted on the back to give the eyes their colour. Eyes made of coloured glass were also used. When glass eyes broke, however, they had sharp edges, and the wire shanks used to fix them posed a further threat to children. It is not uncommon to find that an older bear's eyes have been removed by an anxious parent, and many were simply lost. Sometimes, buttons or stitched eyes replace them.

Plastic eyes were used from the 1950s onwards. Some early ones were still fixed in position with a wire shank, but these were gradually replaced by safety eyes, in which a metal washer locked onto the plastic shank of the eyes.

A variety of materials have been used to stuff bears. Manufacturers often simply made use of anything that was available at the time. Even trimmings from the bears' own mohair fur have sometimes found their way into the stuffing.

The earliest bears were generally stuffed with wood wool (also called excelsior) which is made up of wood shavings of the kind once commonly used to pack china and glass. Bears stuffed with this are often quite heavy and very hard, and will feel crunchy when squeezed.

British bears soon started to become lighter and softer. Kapok, a stuffing made from the seed pods of a tropical tree, was popular with many British manufacturers, although wood wool was sometimes added to give extra firmness where required.

During wartime shortages, virtually any suitable material was pressed into service to be used as stuffing for teddy bears. As stuffing can become displaced by constant hugging or unfortunate accidents, parents would sometimes add extra filling — using anything that came conveniently to hand. Newspapers, nylons, table-cloths, horse hair, rabbit straw and balls of wool are just a few of the things that have been found when bears have been opened up for repair!

When washable bears started to appear in the 1950s, light-weight foam chippings were often used as these could be immersed in water. But these were prone to deteriorate over time, leaving a glutinous mess inside a very flat and limp-looking bear! Foam chippings were gradually replaced by the polyester fillings in wide use today, although wood wool is still used for some traditional bears.

A more recent innovation has been the use of tiny plastic pellets in some bears — especially those made by teddy bear artists. Pellets give wonderfully floppy and posable bears, but can make larger bears extremely heavy. Metal shot is also sometimes used, although its weight means that it is usually only found in very small bears.

Hand-stitched noses and mouths are common on both old and new bears. Many manufacturers have produced bears with open mouths — sometimes complete with an opening and closing mechanism. Occasionally the open mouths contain teeth, but as these bears can look rather fierce, they don't seem to have been very popular with children.

Sealing wax, tin, leather, felt and plastic are just some of the materials which have been used to make noses. Some modern bears have safety noses made of plastic, fixed in the same way as the plastic safety eyes, but most are hand-stitched, and the style of nose and mouth gives the bear much of its character. Some artists develop very individual noses for their bears, which become a kind of 'signature'.

It didn't take long before teddy bears started to find a voice. Squeakers were fitted into some early bears, but more realistic growlers were quickly developed. These were worked first by squeezing or by pulling a string and later by simply tilting the bear. Tilt growlers are still widely used today, although the mechanism used to produce the sound has changed over the years.

Punch growlers were common in British bears, who often have a bare patch where they have been thumped repeatedly in the stomach. In 1907-8 Steiff tried, without much success, to develop a growler which would produce the words 'teddy bear'.

In the 1920s musical boxes were inserted into bears, and more recently, battery-operated talking bears of various kinds have appeared. These bears sometimes have tapes enabling them to tell stories, repeat anything said to them, or even to hold quite convincing conversations with their young owners!

M any early manufacturers did not label their soft toys, or they used only paper tags which were soon removed or destroyed. Others have used a variety of devices to identify their bears.

The best-known manufacturer's label is Steiff's Button in ear. Metal buttons have been inserted into the left ear of all Steiff bears since 1904, and the device was patented in 1905. Initially, the buttons were blank, but new ones showing a small elephant with an S-shaped trunk were soon introduced. Since 1905, buttons carrying the name Steiff have been used.

Several other manufacturers also used buttons of various types to identify their bears, but for only for a limited period — among them Britain's Merrythought, Chad Valley and Dean's. Early bears by the German company Bing were identified by a small arrow-shaped tag in their right ears – later replaced by a button in the left side and then a metal tag on the bear's right arm, after objections from Steiff.

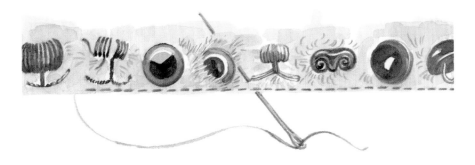

Cloth labels were stitched onto many bears. Sometimes these were attached to a foot pad, while others were inserted into a seam. Paper, plastic or metal 'swing tags' have also frequently been stitched (or more recently stapled) to bears' chests. As these are usually removed before the bear is given to a child, it is rare to find an older bear with its original tag.

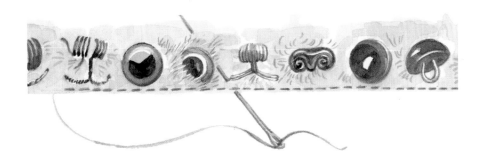

Although some mechanisation has been introduced into soft toy factories, the manufacture of traditional teddy bears still involves a great deal of hand work. In fact, the steps involved have changed remarkably little over the years.

First comes the cutting out. Some of this is now carried out by machine, but longer pile fabrics — especially those used for collectors bears — may still be cut by hand. It is not unusual for a traditional bear to contain around 20 pieces, or more. Body, arm and leg seams must then be stitched, and the head pieces (including the ears) stitched together.

Eyes are inserted. The head and limbs must be stuffed, and these are then attached to the body by means of cotter pin joints. Then the body is stuffed and the final seam closed before a skilled finisher adds the all-important nose and mouth to give the bear its facial expression. Claws may be added, and markings may be airbrushed onto the fur. The bear is then thoroughly brushed and inspected before any clothes and accessories are added.

IT TAKES MORE THAN FIFTEEN DIFFERENT

PRODUCTION STAGES TO MAKE A STEIFF

BEAR, INVOLVING UP TO THIRTY DIFFERENT

EMPLOYEES. EVEN THE EYES ARE POLISHED!

To make your own 9cm (3½ in) traditional bear, you will need:

Materials

1 Small piece of mohair with 4 mm (⅛ in) pile, or upholstery velvet or other fabric of your choice.

2 Tiny piece of leather or ultrasuede for pads.

3 Two black beads for eyes.

4 Thread to match fur plus black thread for nose and mouth.

5 Stuffing (cotton wool would suffice).

6 Five sets of cotter pin joints (available by mail order from suppliers of bear-making components).

7 Scraps of ribbon or lace to trim.

Tools

Small embroidery scissors

Needle

Narrow-nosed pliers (for turning cotter pins in the joints)

Stuffing stick (such as a small wooden nailcare stick)

General guidelines

1 Always place the right sides of the fabric together before stitching.

2 Tack the pieces first with a tiny running stitch, then use a strong back stitch for the permanent seams.

3 Make sure the stuffing goes right into the extremities.

4 After turning and stuffing, close each piece with ladder stitch. 'Invisible' thread is useful here.

To cut out:

1 Trace the pattern pieces and transfer to card.

2 Make sure that the pile of the fabric runs downward, as indicated by the arrows, before placing the pattern pieces on the back of the fabric. Cut out.

To make the bear's head:

1 Tack and backstitch from A down to B.

2 Position the gusset with a tacking stitch at A.

3 Sew from A round to C on one side of the gusset and then on the other, leaving the neck edge B to C open for stuffing the head.

4 Join two ear pieces together by sewing round the curve, leaving the straight edge open between D and D for turning. Turn the ear and then close the opening. Repeat for second ear.

To make the body:

1 Sew the curved edges together between E and F.

2 Join the back pieces to the front from G to F.

3 Stitch from H to F, leaving an opening as indicated.

To make the arms (2):

1 Sew paw pad to inner arm along straight edge.

2 Join inner arm to outer arm, leaving an opening as indicated.

To make the legs (2):

1 With right sides together, sew around the legs from the toe to the back of the heel, leaving an opening as shown. Do not sew across the straight lower edge of the foot.

2 Fit the foot pad, catching it in place at toe and heel before tacking and then stitching.

To make up the bear:

1 Stuff head.

2 Place cotter pin joint in neck opening and close with running stitch.

3 Position joints in arms and legs.

4 Stuff limbs.

5 Close openings in limbs with ladder stitch.

6 Attach head and limbs to body using the cotter pin joints.

7 Stuff body and close opening.

8 Sew ears in position with firm ladder stitch.

9 Sew in eyes and stitch nose and mouth.

10 Trim with lace or ribbon as desired.

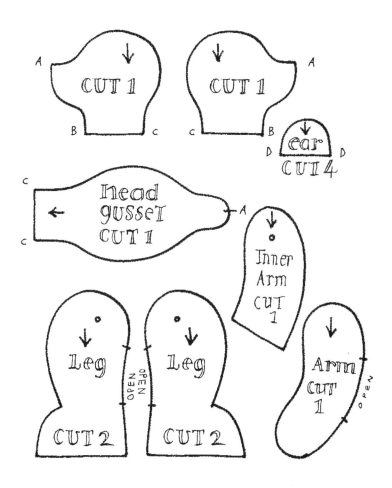

A

CUT 1

B   C

CUT 1

C   B
A

D ear D
CUT 4

C
head
gusset
CUT 1
A
C

Inner
Arm
cut
1

Leg

Leg

OPEN OPEN

CUT 2

CUT 2

Arm
Cut
1

OPEN

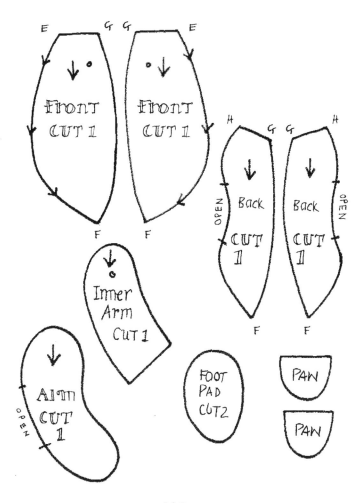

Teddy bears have a number of natural enemies, including household pets and pests, water and excessive heat. Many a bear has been injured by the family dog or by over-zealous washing, and fur will fade if left for long periods in bright sunlight.

Young children should be dissuaded from trimming the fur of collectable bears in the belief that it will grow back! All bears should also be kept well away from older brothers with catapults or worse, as they have a nasty tendency to use beloved bears for target practice.

Regular brushing is essential to keep teddy bears dust free; they can also be vacuumed gently, but place some fine gauze over the nozzle to prevent any loose bits of bear being accidentally sucked up! Very dirty bears should be cleaned more thoroughly, as dirt left in the fabric will cause it to deteriorate and may attract pests.

The cleaning of fragile old bears is probably best left to the professionals, but if the fabric is in good condition, it can be wiped gently with the foam created when a gentle liquid detergent — the kind used to wash delicate fabrics — is whisked up. This should be applied only to the surface of the bear, taking care to ensure that the stuffing does not become wet. All traces of detergent should be carefully removed with a damp cloth, before the bear is left in a warm place to dry. When dry, the fur should be gently brushed.

Bears should be inspected regularly to make sure that they are free from pests. Look for the papery casings left by moths, for small round holes, especially in the paw pads, or for the tiny white larvae which are the signs that your bear has unwelcome guests.

A popular method of treatment is to seal the bear securely in a polythene bag and pop him in the freezer for a couple of days — ignoring the pathetic looks every time you reach for the frozen peas! This method doesn't guarantee a complete cure: placing the bear in a sealed polythene bag with some moth balls or suitable insecticide for 24–48 hours may be more effective. Never spray the bear himself with insecticide.

Simple repairs can be carried out at home if a few basic techniques are learnt, although major repairs to a valuable bear are best left to the professionals, who can work miracles with even the most accident-prone of teddies.

Many bear-making books show how to insert glass eyes, how to use ladder stitch to close seams and attach ears, and how to stitch noses and mouths. In fact, making a bear or two can be a very good way to practise techniques before starting on your own repairs.

CHAPTER SIX

teddy miscellany

The British journal *The Veterinary Record* once published a paper on the diseases suffered by *Brunus edwardii* (species nova) – otherwise known as the teddy bear. Among the many syndromes found were 'coagulation and clumping of stuffing', loss of limbs (apparently often the result of disputed ownership), alopecia, ocular conditions (such as a lopsided squint), and emotional disturbances apparently caused by a lack of love. The researchers also noted that 98% of the bears were jaundiced, but eventually concluded that the yellow colour was probably normal!

According to a recent study, it's adults, not very young children, who like their teddies cute and cuddly. Four-year-old children were found to prefer bears with more adult features while those aged six and eight years went for the more baby-like bears. It was concluded that the development of the teddy from the long-nosed, long-limbed creatures of the earliy years to the more friendly snub-nosed bears of today reflected the tastes of the parents buying the bears rather than those of their children.

Teddy bears have turned up in the law courts on numerous occasions – one even helped to send two car thieves to jail. Bears themselves have been the victims of mass bearnapping, and more than one teddy has found himself bearsonally involved in divorce proceedings. In Britain a company director even plastered the area around his former home with hundreds of posters demanding the return of his bears, after his wife named two of them in her divorce petition. She was unrepentant, claiming that he felt more for these 'other women' than he did for her

Teddy bears are always the height of fashion. They appear on dress fabrics and sweaters; tiny, fully jointed bears are turned into brooches and pendants; they've graced hats at Ascot — and one German countess was photographed with at least a dozen cuddly bears decorating the neckline of her black gown! Perhaps the most outrageous use of teddies in fashion, however, were the fake fur jackets made from teddy bears by designer Jean Charles de Castelbajac. They were the stars of the Paris catwalks in 1988.

American Russell McLean became known as the Teddy Bear Man after telling a local radio station how he wanted to raise funds to buy teddy bears to give to children on their first frightening night in hospital. He presented his fifty thousandth bear shortly before ill health forced him to give up this work.

Today the international organisation Good Bears of the World follows his example — donating bears not only to children but to anyone who would benefit from the comfort a teddy can bring. Many are sent to children's hospitals, but bears are also frequently requested by hospices, who have witnessed the enormous comfort

they give not only to the patient but also to the family left behind. Some police forces use Good Bears when talking to the young victims of abuse, and in some countries they are carried in ambulances to bring immediate comfort to accident victims.

A bear called Sir Koff a Lot is given to many hospital patients following open-heart surgery. Patients need to clear the congestion in their lungs, and in the past would have hugged a pillow or blanket to their chests to help ease the pain of coughing. Now they hug the specially designed teddy bears, which have proved as popular with adults as they are with children.

In June 1990 a sad one-eyed furless fellow, almost unrecognisable as a bear, came under the hammer at a London auction house. When the auctioneer asked for an opening bid, there was not even a ripple of interest. He suggested a lower sum, and then a lower one, until he was asking for a bid of just £10. Still no one was interested. Finally, a hand went up in the front row, a voice called out "I'll give you a fiver", and the hammer quickly fell.

It was the bear's lucky day, for the bidder was Peter Fagan, creator of the Colour Box range of miniature resin teddy bears – modelled from real teddies. Peter's wife Frances and their daughter Lucy took the new arrival under their wings, stuffed him with rabbit straw, covered his missing eye with a jaunty eye patch, and dressed him in a smart sailor's uniform. They called him Captain Arthur Crown (although he had actually cost forty times more than an English half a crown) and he went on to become one of the most popular members of the Colour Box teddy collection – much in demand for personal appearances.

A STAR-STRUCK BEAR CALLED TIDDLES BUILT UP AN IMPRESSIVE PHOTOGRAPH ALBUM BY STOWING AWAY IN THE SUITCASE WHEN HIS GUARDIAN, FILM CAMERAMAN ANTHONY SHEARN, TRAVELLED THE WORLD ON LOCATION. THE BATTERED FLOPPY-EARED TED CUDDLED UP TO KIRI TE KANAWA, SIR PAUL MCCARTNEY, SIR ANTHONY QUAYLE, RICK WAKEMAN, JENNY AGUTTER AND A HOST OF OTHER ACTORS AND MUSICIANS, AS WELL AS POSING FOR PICTURES AT EGYPT'S PYRAMIDS, AGAINST THE NEW YORK SKYLINE, IN INDONESIA, SINGAPORE AND A HOST OF OTHER COUNTRIES.

Intrepid teddy bears have been taken on expeditions and into war zones, they have travelled in hot air balloons, made solo flights, dived to the bottom of the sea, parachuted out of aircraft, and have even taken part in bungy jumping contests. One small teddy who took part in a sponsored parachute jump in Wales managed to go missing for a full six months after jumping with 95 other teddies from an aircraft. He was only rescued when an instructor at the parachute club landed off-target himself and found the bear lying in the grass.

In the 1980s, regular Teddy Bear Concerts were introduced at London's Barbican concert hall. Teddies were invited to join in by 'dancing' in time to the music and by being thrown in the air to show that they were enjoying themselves. Naturally this resulted in some bears taking dramatic tumbles from the balcony. But arrangements were made for lost bears to be collected and brought to the stage, so that they could be reunited with their owners in the interval.

It has been reported that more than 40% of children simply name their bears Teddy. Other popular names include Ted and Edward. The Roosevelt connection has led to large numbers of Theodores and Theos.

The bear's appearance may also provide inspiration for his name — Tubby, Podge, Fluffy, Curly and Woolly, for instance. Others are named after well-known characters like Pooh, Paddington and Rupert, even if they bear little resemblance to their literary namesakes.

Many other bears are named after their place of origin. There is an abundance of Kensingtons, for instance, since major teddy bear fairs have been held in that London borough for a number of years. Others take their names from a tradename spotted on their original label. Hugmee is frequent among Chiltern Hugmee bears, while many a Dean's bear has been christened Dean, and Merry is common amongst Merrythoughts.

NEARLY A CENTURY AFTER THE FIRST TEDDY BEAR, HE REMAINS AS POPULAR AS EVER — NOT JUST WITH CHILDREN BUT WITH ADULTS AS WELL. HIS NEW ROLE AS A COLLECTABLE MAY HAVE WON HIM EVEN MORE CONVERTS. BUT HIS APPEAL IS TOTALLY INDEPENDENT OF HIS MONETARY VALUE OR INVESTMENT POTENTIAL — AND ALL THE MORE ENDURING AS A RESULT.

Published by MQ Publications Limited
254-258 Goswell Road, London EC1V 7EB

Copyright © MQ Publications Limited 1998

Text © Pat Rush 1998
Illustrations © Isobel Bushell 1998
Teddy bear pattern © Wendy Sue Wilkinson 1998

ISBN: 1-897954-21-2

1 3 5 7 9 0 8 6 4 2

Designed by Alison Shackleton

Printed and bound in Italy